Petals of the Moon:

A Journal for Dreamers

C. Churchill

Petals of the Moon: A Journal for Dreamers

Copyright 2019 C. Churchill

Journal inspired by "Petals of the Moon"

Cover by C. Churchill

Also, by C. Churchill:

Petals of the Moon: A Poetry Collection

Wildflower Tea: A Poetry Collection

Wildflower Tea: A Journal for Daydreamers

Color Body Feels

I am a Woman not a Winston

C. Churchill on social media:

Instagram @cc_writes

Facebook @cchurchillwrites

Petals of the Moon is a collection of poetry written by based on emotions and events of the night. I often write what I dream. I also write when I cannot sleep.

The concept for this journal is to write when you are experiencing a restlessness at night.

Unfurl your petals, bloom into your creativity!

So, you have this journal in your grubby little paws and it feels amazing! I don't know about you, but I love a new journal.

As a writer and artist, I have hundreds of journals and sketchbooks everywhere.

So, one day I was thinking...

...

...

...

Sorry I was thinking.

Anyhoo.

Back on track I was thinking wouldn't it be fun to make a journal where you could write or draw anything?

Alas those are notebooks and sketchbooks.

This journal has a twist. It is an eclectic mix of prompts, blank pages, free writing, doodle days and what I call Brain Starters.

Choose what you like and date what you like. This is your sacred space.

A Brain Starter is an incomplete thought, a choose your ending type prompt.

So, are you ready for some fun?

It is OK to have fun while writing.

Let your pen take you on an adventure.

Need to know info!

Brain Starter: What comes next? The choice is yours.

Free Write: Go for it!! Journal freely.

Prompt: Write or Draw anything related to the prompt, or even do both!

Doodle Day: Let your pen freely move about the pages and get some shapes in there.

This journal is yours, kind of like a child. Does it have a name?

Captains Log: Brain Starter

Entry 01:

Abruptly I woke to find a pen in my hand and a book lay open on the night stand...

Captains Log: Free Write

Entry 02:

Fill the pages

Here are some suggestions:

Dreams

Poems

Wishes

Letters

Doodles

Drawings

Shopping lists

Reasons you are amazing

Keep going....

Captains Log: Prompt

Entry 03:

If you were to plant a garden what would you grow?

Captains Log: Doodle Day

Entry 04:

If you are at all wondering why I chose Captains Log, Moon, Space, Time Travel, Dreams, you know...It just fit. This is an adventure after all.

Captains Log: Brain Starter

Entry 05:

I was walking home from school and out of the corner of my eye I saw a giant flash of bright pink fur. I could only assume...

If you don't fill the pages with the prompts, then doodle on it! Or doodle while you draw, or don't doodle. It is your adventure.

Captains Log: Free Write

Entry 06:

And yes of course you write in this like a journal as well.
Don't be silly you know I am not a fan of rules.

Captains Log: Prompt

Entry 07:

If there was anything you could have right this second, what would it be?

Captains Log: Doodle Day

Entry 08:

Captains Log: Brain Starter

Entry 09:

I never noticed how the man behind the counter only had eight fingers, I once heard he...

Are you feeling inspired?

Are you feeling risky?

I hope so.

Writing and drawing prompts are a fun way to think outside of the normal box. I have used drawing prompts in my art classes as a teacher and it has helped my students relax their minds and warm up their creative side.

Captains Log: Free Write

Entry 10:

Captains Log: Prompt

Entry 11:

What would you wish for?

Captains Log: Doodle Day

Entry 12:

Captains Log: Free Write

Entry 13:

Captains Log: Brain Starter

Entry 14:

I was crouched under the picnic table eating the last of the...

Captains Log: Prompt

Entry 15:

What was your last dream?

Captains Log: Doodle Day

Entry 14:

Captains Log: Free Write

Entry 15:

Captains Log: Brain Starter

Entry 16:

I heard a knock at the door, right away I knew it must be...

Captains Log: Prompt

Entry 17:

What is the strangest thing you have eaten?

Captains Log: Doodle Day

Entry 18:

They say it takes 30 days to make a habit or break a habit.

I don't know if it is true, but it seems legit.

Captains Log: Free Write

Entry 19:

Captains Log: Brain Starter

Entry 20:

When I walked back into the room, they looked at me like
I was crazy. I guess it was because...

Captains Log: Prompt

Entry 21

What is the last gift you gave yourself? Why?

81

Captains Log: Free Write

Entry 22:

Captains Log: Doodle Day

Entry 23:

Captains Log: Brain Starter

Entry 24:

I couldn't recall where I was, the room was black and all I could hear was...

Captains Log: Prompt

Entry 25:

Describe in detail the last time you saw someone you
loved.

Captains Log: Free Write

Entry 26:

Captains Log: Doodle Day

Entry 27

Remember these blank pages are supposed to be filled. Even if you just write the same word thirty times to fill fill fill fill fill fill fill fill fill fill fill fill fill fill fill fill fill fill fill fill fill fill fill fill fill fill fill fill fill fill fill it.

Did you count? I did 29 on purpose.

Captains Log: Brain Starter

Entry 28:

There was no key, but I knew I had to get in. I looked
around and did not see anyone so I...

Captains Log: Prompt

Entry 29:

If there was no social media how would you stay in contact with those you love? Write them a letter and tell them how you feel.

Write a few letters.

Maybe even send them. People love getting snail mail.

Or don't. Its up to you. Your adventure, do as you wish.

So why you may ask did I say write a letter to the ones you love? Simple enough we store emotions in places that sometimes it is much easier to write about than say. Even if you never show these feelings to anyone it is nice to get them out.

So, I hope these pages are becoming filled! A journal for Dreamers is for those who maybe have been told their head is in the clouds. I will tell you a secret, those are my favorite kind of people.

Captains Log: Free Write

Entry 30:

Never be afraid to fill the page. You can always edit later.

Captains Log: Last entry

Entry 31:

Write a letter to your younger self. Let them know how much you love them. Let them know it is ok to dream.

Journal now, edit later.

Keeping journals for reference is a great way to start new creative writing projects.

Also available for writers

Wildflower Tea: A Journal for Daydreamers. Keep those observation skills in tune with this writer's journal.

Keep on keeping on.

Much love,

C. Churchill

Made in the USA
Lexington, KY
25 April 2019